The Wonder of
BALD EAGLES

Adapted from Charlene Gieck's *Bald Eagle Magic for Kids*
by Eileen Foran
Photography by Tom & Pat Leeson

Gareth Stevens Publishing
MILWAUKEE

For a free color catalog describing Gareth Stevens' list of high-quality books, call 1-800-341-3569 (USA) or 1-800-461-9120 (Canada).

Library of Congress Cataloging-in-Publication Data

Foran, Eileen.
    The wonder of bald eagles / adapted from Charlene Gieck's Bald eagle magic for kids by Eileen Foran; photography by Tom Leeson and Pat Leeson.
        p.   cm. — (Animal wonders)
    Includes index.
    Summary: Text and photographs introduce that valiant bird of prey, the bald eagle.
    ISBN 0-8368-0854-1
    1. Bald eagle—Juvenile literature. [1. Bald eagle. 2. Eagles.] I. Leeson, Tom, ill. II. Leeson, Pat, ill. III. Gieck, Charlene. Bald eagle magic for kids. IV. Title. V. Series.
    QL696.F32F67   1992
    598.9'6—dc20   92-16943

North American edition first published in 1992 by
Gareth Stevens Publishing
1555 North RiverCenter Drive, Suite 201
Milwaukee, WI 53212, USA

This U.S. edition is abridged from *Bald Eagle Magic for Kids,* copyright © 1991 by NorthWord Press, Inc., and written by Charlene Gieck, first published in 1991 by NorthWord Press, Inc., and published in a library edition by Gareth Stevens, Inc. Additional end matter copyright © 1992 by Gareth Stevens, Inc.

Cover design: Kristi Ludwig

Printed in the United States of America

1 2 3 4 5 6 7 8 9 98 97 96 95 94 93 92

But you never were made, as I,
On the wings of the wind to fly!
The eagle said.

— Will Carlton

The bald eagle is a strong
and beautiful bird. It is
the symbol of the United
States, where it is seen
on posters and money.

The white feathers on its head and dark brown feathers on its body make the bald eagle easy to see — even when it is soaring miles overhead.

The bald eagle gets its name from an Old English word, "balde," which means "white."

By age five, all bald eagles
have a white head and tail.
At this age, they are ready
to have their own families.

While the adult bald eagle
is easy to recognize, the
young bald eagle looks like
a golden eagle or a hawk.

The bald eagle has a wing-span of seven to eight feet. Female eagles are bigger than males.

Eagles may seem big because of their many layers of feathers. But their hollow bones make them lightweight for flying.

Eagles are *birds of prey*.
This means that they
eat meat.

Eagles like fish most of all.
But they also eat geese,
ducks, rabbits, turtles, and
carrion. They eat carrion
mostly in the winter, when
other food is hard to find.

When an eagle spots a fish in the water, it will swoop down and catch the fish with its feet. An eagle may also try stealing food from other birds of prey.

An eagle sees very well.
It can spot a rabbit from
two miles away!

An eagle's *talons*, or
claws, are curved and
razor-sharp for catching
and holding its prey.
The rough bumps on an
eagle's toes help it hold
slippery, wriggling fish.

Male and female eagles *court* each other in early spring. After courting, both birds help build a nest. When it is first built, the nest may be as big as three feet wide and three feet deep. Each year, the eagles add more sticks, and so the nest gets bigger and bigger each year.

The largest eagle nest ever found was nine feet wide and twelve feet deep. That's probably bigger than your bedroom!

Eagles usually nest in trees
near rivers or lakes. They
will always choose a tree
that is taller than the other
trees around it.

The female eagle lays one
to three eggs in the spring.
She sits on the eggs to
keep them warm and safe.
When the eggs hatch, out
come tiny *eaglets,* covered
with thick *down.*

The adult eagles are kept
very busy finding food for
their baby eagles.

When eaglets are about
three weeks old, they get
brown feathers. Eating,
sleeping, and caring for
their feathers is about all
they do at this age.

Eaglets begin *fledging,* or becoming ready for their first flight, when they are about three weeks old.

Eagles start to hunt for their own food soon after they learn to fly. They are now called *immatures*.

Bald eagles are found only in North America. They live near lakes and rivers where there are many trees and few people. If a human gets too close, an adult eagle may leave the nest, and the young eagles may become chilled and die.

It's fine to watch eagles, but only from a distance. Winter is a great time to watch eagles. Many people watch eagles from their cars or use binoculars instead of trying to get too close to an eagle's nest.

There are four types of eagles — sea eagles, booted eagles, serpent eagles, and buteonine (pronounced BYOO-tee-uh-nine) eagles.

Sea eagles have dark and white feathers. They live near rivers, lakes, and seas. The bald eagle is part of this group.

Booted eagles have brown feathers down to their toes.   They live on wooded and barren mountains. The golden eagle is in this group.

Serpent eagles have short tails. Their short legs are covered with scales. They live in tropical grasslands.

Buteonine eagles are big and strong. The peaks on their crested heads make them look like witches. They live in tropical jungles.

The bald eagle is an *endangered* animal.
People are the eagle's biggest enemy.

Eagles need peace and quiet. But people cut down tall trees for lumber and crowd the lakeshores. This destroys the eagles' home.

Many people are trying
to help keep eagles alive
and well. In the United
States, a law protects
eagles from people who
want to harm them.

By protecting eagles,
we are helping to save
a bird that is beautiful
and important.

Glossary

birds of prey – birds that hunt animals and eat their flesh

carrion – dead and rotting animal flesh

court – to perform actions that will attract an animal of the opposite sex for mating

down – soft, fluffy feathers

eaglets – young eagles

endangered – in danger of becoming extinct, or of no longer existing

fledging – growing feathers for flying

immatures – young eagles ready to hunt and take care of themselves

talons – the sharp claws of a bird of prey

Index